curious?about

BARBIE

I0896480

BY RACHEL GRACK

AMICUS LEARNING

What are you

curious about?

Curious About is published by
Amicus Learning, an imprint of Amicus
P.O. Box 227, Mankato, MN 56002
www.amicuspublishing.us

Copyright © 2026 Amicus.
International copyright reserved in all countries.
No part of this book may be reproduced in any
form without written permission from the publisher.

Editors: Ana Brauer and Grace Cain
Series Designer: Kathleen Petelinsek
Book Designer and Photo Researcher: Sara Hood

Library of Congress Cataloging-in-Publication Data
Names: Koestler-Grack, Rachel A., 1973–author.
Title: Curious about Barbie / by Rachel Grack.
Description: Mankato, MN : Amicus Learning, an imprint of Amicus, [2026] | Series: Curious about favorite brands | Includes bibliographical references and index. | Audience: Ages 6–9 | Audience: Grades 2–3 | Summary: "Who invented Barbie dolls? Spark elementary readers' curiosity about the popular toy brand's history, products and movies, and cultural impact with insightful questions and well-researched answers. Includes table of contents, glossary, further resources, and index"—Provided by publisher.
Identifiers: LCCN 2024050042 (print) | LCCN 2024050043 (ebook) | ISBN 9798892005104 (library binding) | ISBN 9798892005647 (paperback) | ISBN 9798892006187 (ebook)
Subjects: LCSH: Barbie dolls—Juvenile literature. | Barbie dolls—History—Juvenile literature.
Classification: LCC NK4894.3.B37 K64 2026 (print) | LCC NK4894.3.B37 (ebook) | DDC 688.7/221—dc23/eng/20241214
LC record available at https://lccn.loc.gov/2024050042
LC ebook record available at https://lccn.loc.gov/2024050043

Photo Credits: Airbnb/unknown, 13; Alamy Stock Photo/ Bob London, 9, Chuck Mason, 17, FlixPix, 2, 11, Malcolm Park, 2, 5, NASA Photo, 3, 19, Sipa USA, 15; Getty Images/ Bettmann, 6, Vicky Kasala Productions, 7, Wiktor Szymanowicz, 12; Shutterstock/NightGliderSA, 15, Savanevich Viktar, cover; Mattel, Inc/unknown, 8, 9, 15, 16, 18, 20, 21

Every effort has been made to contact copyright holders for material reproduced in this book. Any omissions will be rectified in subsequent printings if notice is given to the publisher.

Printed in India

CHAPTER ONE

How old is Barbie?

Her birthday is March 9, 1959. This was the day the toy company Mattel introduced her to the world. Barbie became one of the most successful toy **brands** in history. Today, the character is in many books, shows, and movies.

The first Barbie doll wore a striped swimsuit.

Paper dolls were popular from the 1930s through the 1950s.

Who invented the Barbie doll?

Ruth Handler came up with the idea in 1959. Her daughter liked playing with paper dolls. Handler wanted to sell a real doll that looked like the paper ones. Handler named the doll after her daughter, Barbara.

Ruth Handler thought dolls were a good way for kids to play and learn.

When did Ken come along?

Barbie was alone for two years. Then in 1961, Mattel released the Ken Carson doll. The company made up a story about them. They said that the dolls met while shooting a **commercial** together. It was love at first sight. They share the same hometown of Willows, Wisconsin.

1961 1971 1983

KEN AND BARBIE OVER THE YEARS

Ken has had more than 100 looks since 1961.

DID YOU KNOW?
Handler named Ken after her son.

1992

2010

2023

CHAPTER TWO

2

What is the World of Barbie?

Barbie became very popular. Mattel created more characters and toys. It became a whole world for Barbie and her friends. The products came to life through cartoons and movies. Kids began collecting the dolls and toys. They watched their favorite characters on TV.

Barbie (2023) was an instant hit.

HI, BARBIE!

There are many cartoon Barbie movies. In 2023, the first live action movie came out. *Barbie* made $1.45 billion worldwide!

Where does Barbie live?

The first Barbie Dreamhouse came out in 1962.

The character lives in Malibu, California. Her most famous home is the Barbie Dreamhouse. There have been 20 different styles. The first was a fold-out **studio apartment**. Today, it is a three-story **mansion**. It has a pool and an elevator.

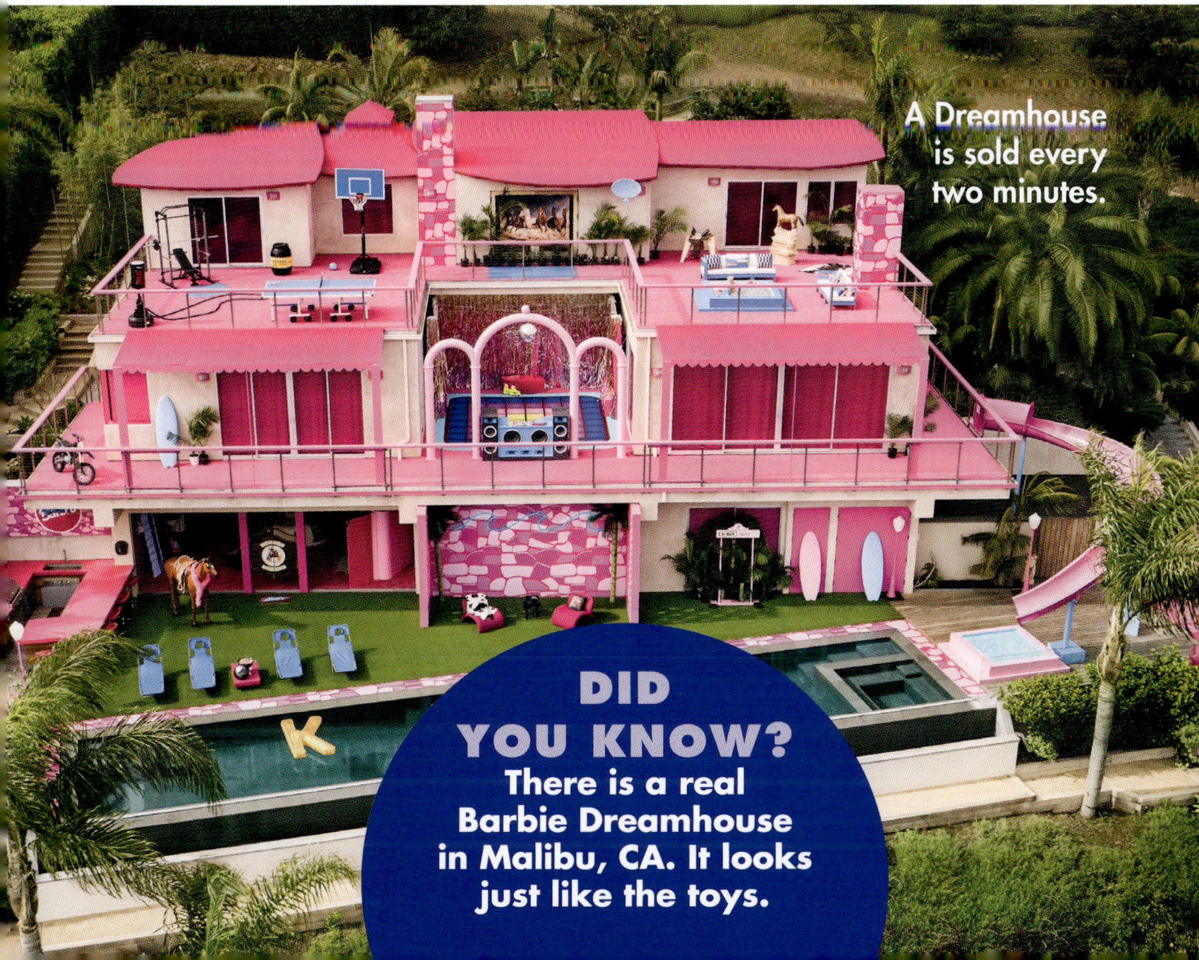

A Dreamhouse is sold every two minutes.

DID YOU KNOW?
There is a real Barbie Dreamhouse in Malibu, CA. It looks just like the toys.

How big is the Barbie family?

Over the years, Mattel gave Barbie several family members. Many of the dolls have been **discontinued**. Today, she has three younger sisters. Skipper is Barbie's teenage sister. Stacie is a little younger. Six-year-old Chelsea is the youngest. Their parents are George and Margaret Roberts.

ROBERTS FAMILY TREE

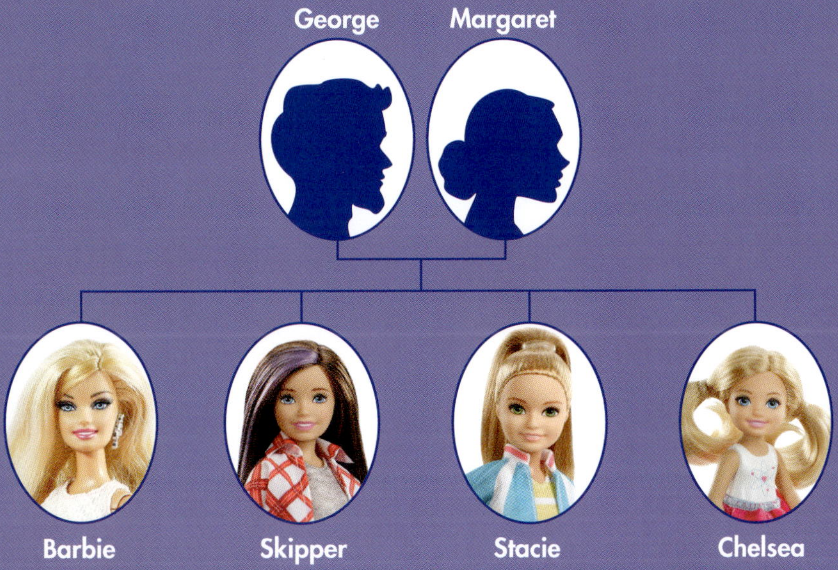

Mattel makes new Barbie products every year.

Who is Barbie's best friend?

Playing with dolls is a great way to be creative with your friends.

Midge Hadley has been her BFF since 1963. Mattel quickly made more friends for Barbie. Christie was the first Black doll in 1968. Her character was later renamed Nikki. Some friend characters stuck around. Others only stayed for a short time. Just like in real life!

CHAPTER THREE

How many jobs has Barbie had?

1961—Singer

1965—Astronaut

1973—Surgeon

1985—Veterinarian

1991—Naval Petty Officer

1999—Airline Pilot

2004—Presidential Candidate

2016—Game Developer

2019—Marine Biologist

More than 250! Her first job was a model. She is also a doctor, police officer, and race car driver. Barbie's many jobs **inspire** kids to think big and go far. Barbie has even been all the way to space! This helped girls become interested in **STEM**.

Two astronaut Barbies spent time on the International Space Station (ISS) in 2022.

Is there a Barbie who looks like me?

In April 2023, Mattel introduced a doll with Down Syndrome.

Probably! Barbie comes in 35 skin tones. She has nine body types. Some dolls wear glasses or hearing aids. Others use a wheelchair. It is part of Barbie **Diversity**. This means Barbie is for everyone. Barbie is you and whoever you dream of being.

35 SKIN TONES

9 BODY TYPES

97 HAIRSTYLES

REPRESENTING DISABILITIES

STAY CURIOUS!

ASK MORE QUESTIONS

How many Barbie movies are there?

Can I stay in the real Barbie Dreamhouse?

Try a BIG QUESTION: What new career could Barbie try?

SEARCH FOR ANSWERS

Search the library catalog or the Internet.
A librarian, teacher, or parent can help you.

Using Keywords
Find the looking glass.

Keywords are the most important words in your question.

If you want to know about:

- the number of Barbie movies, type: BARBIE MOVIES
- how you can stay at the Barbie Dreamhouse, type: RENT BARBIE DREAMHOUSE

FIND GOOD SOURCES

Here are some good, safe sources you can use in your research.
Your librarian can help you find more.

Books

Barbie Dolls
by Nathan Sommer, 2022.

Barbie
by Rachel First, 2025.

Internet Sites

Barbie on YouTube: You Can Be Anything
https://www.youtube.com/playlist?list=PL5BsRl9zFaeTTpR7JiTY389R31NV2-M6T
Barbie inspires viewers to dream big through inspiring role models.

Mattel: Barbie
https://kids.mattel.com/barbie
Visit Mattel's Barbie website for videos, games, and coloring sheets.

Every effort has been made to ensure that these websites are appropriate for children. However, because of the nature of the Internet, it is impossible to guarantee that these sites will remain active indefinitely or that their contents will not be altered.

SHARE AND TAKE ACTION

Make a Barbie movie.
Use dolls to act out a story and record it.

Design a doll.
Create your own Barbie character.

Talk about how Barbie inspires girls to achieve their dreams.

GLOSSARY

brand A group of products owned by the same company.

commercial A television advertisement.

discontinue When a product is no longer available or made.

diversity The practice of including all kinds of people.

inspire To motivate a person to want to do something.

mansion A large and fancy house.

STEM A group of careers that use science, technology, engineering, and mathematics.

studio apartment A one-room apartment that includes a bedroom, kitchen, and living room with a separate bathroom.

INDEX

About the Author

Rachel Grack has been editing and writing children's books since 1999. She lives on a small ranch in southern Arizona. As a lover of stories, Disney is close to her heart. She also enjoys watching her grandchildren play Pokémon games on her Nintendo 64 console.